ARMY OF GIANTS

MATHEW ROHRER

SEATTLE

ARMY OF GIANTS

Published by Wave Books
www.wavepoetry.com

Wave Books titles are distributed to the trade by
Consortium Book Sales and Distribution
Phone: 800-283-3572 / SAN 631-760X
Library of Congress Cataloging-in-Publication Data
Names: Rohrer, Matthew, author.
Title: Army of giants / Matthew Rohrer.
Description: First edition. | Seattle : Wave Books, 2024.
Identifiers: LCCN 2024009316 | ISBN 9798891060098 (paperback)
Subjects: LCGFT: Poetry.
Classification: LCC PS3568.O524 A89 2024 | DDC 811/.54—dc23/eng/20240304
LC record available at https://lccn.loc.gov/2024009316
Designed by Crisis
Printed in the United States of America
9 8 7 6 5 4 3 2 1
First Edition
Wave Books 118

ARMY OF THE DEAD

ARMY OF GIANTS

ARMY OF POETS

ARMY OF THE DEAD

PRISONERS

A distant beat comes
from the melting snow.
A delivery truck slowly
backing up. I have been
inside our apartment for centuries!
Trapped on a small blue-
and-green planet, spinning
through space, a prisoner.
But there is no jailor.
Just a cloud that appears
overhead in the shape
of a sword, severing
afternoon from evening.

THE GOOSE LEADER

Mosquitoes being driven indoors
by the cold fringes
of what's to come
tonight in our bedroom
is their last stand
turning to my left
to cradle my heart
I sleep on deeper
air disturbed by sirens
the goose leader honks
flying low through darkness
warning the others don't
hit this sleeping house

WE SHALL OVERCOME

One lone woman protesting
on the traffic island
WE SHALL OVERCOME she
has written in pen
rush hour the cars
honking at each other
without people in them
I walk by her
I try to look
into her eyes she
does not look assured
that we shall overcome
she is a small poem
only you will read

A LONELY TRUMPET

A lonely trumpet mutters
a hawk is screaming
just a few trees
are turning the park
is surrounded by sirens
magical talismans to ward
off calamity are everywhere
walking through leaf shadows
I take her hand
gingerly her shoulder aches
from the stress of
lying awake in America

THE HANDOFF

I wrote a poem
about a Taoist immortal
but I was kidding
I care very little
but I do believe
if there were magic
animals would understand it
then it started raining
and my daughter cheered
and on the stoop
we sat watching our
divorced neighbors' sad handoff
of 2 sleepy kids
in a lighted doorway

DARKENED LIGHTHOUSE

Clouds like feathers exploding
beneath them I walk
the very long walk
to the wine shop
I bypass the election
this afternoon gazing instead
like a darkened lighthouse
on everything and breathing
the fringes of winter
pausing beneath a tree
I never finished reading
the ancient poem explaining
my next move
guessing it said I continue

SUNDAY NIGHT NOTHING'S WORSE

Sunday night nothing's worse
the apartment is silent
but no one's asleep
I'm lying in bed
listening to someone drive
all the way down
Greenwood and then disappear
in reverie I return
to my childhood schoolyard
to some old beefs
that can't be squashed
those kids are dead
wide-eyed in bed I
orbit helplessly the sun

PASSED OVER

Passover and the families
come out like dogwood
blossoms when it's cold
I walk around aimlessly
it's the highest form
of praise or it's
eating dinner on blankets
under the sagacious trees

in childhood I prayed
into the floor vent
that Lucifer consider me
just someone passing by

and I've been spared
in fact I thrive

MY NEIGHBOR

Dingy February I pass
through it like curtains
with nowhere to go
like three red kites
caught in a tree
it's very cold out
how is my neighbor
that's from a haiku
I should look in
on her later tonight
the haiku is called
Don't Be a Fool

AT MY LOWEST POINT

At my lowest point
on the highest point
in Brooklyn the harbor
grey as the sky
standing beside a monument
to a shipwreck horrible
cenotaph with a lifelike
sinking ship and all
the names worn away
to be a person
and not a tree
or a cedar waxwing
feels a little shameful
light snow starts falling

GREENWOOD

The beech tree asks me
to place my hand
on its smooth hide,
I hear it.

I make a path
like a deer through
the uncut hair of graves.

All the headstones say
God Is Love
but everybody here is dead.

BIRTHDAY POEM

Statue of a soldier
who doesn't understand yet
that he has died, his gun
is broken off, a black angel
takes him by the elbow
Come on, she says,
and join the list of names
carved in this stone.
But he's looking off
behind her. Everywhere
the snow is packed and it's still
snowing. Two seagulls fly out
of the snow and return to it
in a moment,
like they are snow.

SWEET DREAMS

Some trees have early
shed their leaves.
Some graves are decorated
for the season.
Some geese batter the fog
with their wings.
A hearse rolls through
a red light because
who even cares.
Onto a heartbreaking headstone
someone carved *Sweet Dreams.*

ARMY OF GIANTS

49

This guy unloading a truck
at the grocery store talking
on a slightly out-of-date
headset with a vehemence
suggesting on the other
end is someone who gets him
and that he is an asshole

I admit I smirk at him
who am I? Oh hello there
welcome to this long poem
written on the coldest day
anyone can remember
follow me into the store
where I show great self-restraint

I only shop from my list
I linger just a little
in front of the seafood case
I hear what sounds like a wolf
or it is ghostly echoes
of all the former live things
arranged in cold pyramids

Gliding down the aisles, for that
is how it feels not breathing
as deeply as I'd like to
I think I hear artichokes
and the flayed wheat in crackers
still crying out, I have read
too many books, and I dream

And in dreams everyone comes
together in a landscape
that's entirely alive
standing by the dream harbor
the sea and the ships on her
and the stone streets are alive

I put in a plastic bag
8 limes, even the plastic
was alive, it used to be
Precambrian vegetables
one of the books I just read
said Nature's just separate things
in my pocket my phone beeps

S. doesn't need a ride home
she's punishing herself for
being unhappy, not me

I like to lie on my back
waiting for the clouds to appear
or walk through the park beneath
an arbor that's in full leaf

The trees circulate tree blood
and send neurological
impulses just like we do
only slowly, so slowly
and in mysterious ways
using their roots the trees speak
and all the other trees nod

Empty shelves in the meat aisle
are a relief, the weather
must have slowed deliveries
and you don't need me to say
what is too easy to say
about animal pieces
stacked up in cold pyramids

The guy from the truck walks by
getting yelled at by his boss
ill-advisedly I look
at his face, there's, in his eyes,
the look of some animal

that's usually quite fierce
but now is wrapped in plastic

▬

Sorry, I had to eat lunch
which gave me a chance to think
more about that last image
I hear the famous German
filmmaker describing bears
in that line, how in their eyes
what you're looking for's not there

Then my body dropped from cold
standing in the checkout line
muttering and head-shaking
I righted myself and paid
white dust lay across the streets
but it hadn't snowed it was
just a prophylactic salting

Driving home the radio
says stay indoors, I'm wearing
gloves the steering wheel's frozen
inside the cemetery
all the bones are extra cold
but they don't care, why would they
they never felt cold like that

And also, where did they go?
I know it's boring to ask
it's somehow beyond our grasp
sitting with my blinker on
waiting to turn left I watch
the bare trees blown by the wind
it's possible they're dreaming

THE WINTER SUN

A cold day is a prison
a little music breaks it open
clouded and angry like a child
let it roll all over me
I know love is the answer
to everyone's question and I know
they aren't listening it is enough
to have this leg across mine
and break open bottles of wine
over the books from the library
while my mind feels like a tide pool
a hopeless case writhing and beautiful
what is wrong is only temporary
if you bend like a weed in a stream

the winter sun is this year
the most annoying it's ever been
at eye level all the way
down the street like a tree
that's particularly obnoxious
at the end of the block
I battle through
my whole face locked against it

walking down Broadway
turning myself sideways
to pass through the beautiful crowd

a truck selling very small cupcakes
has a line standing beside it
I prefer pie
maybe you've read my other poem
it's called PIE
wherein I decide the most tragic thing
about Li Po is no pie
in ancient China
all these people waiting for cupcakes
are blessed imagine their lives
compared to Li Po's
which I do as I walk south on Broadway
they aren't sick shitting their pants
in a camp by the sea
shaking all day in the sun
rattling at night knees drawn up
why do I think of this
the winter sun can't hurt me
the diplomatic corps works for me
while I sleep they fend off
the Arabian king when he says
Cut the head off the snake

I buy wine in the morning
for the night when my love
sits beside me on the couch
kind of manic the cold air
curling on itself outside the windows

My face breaks into a smile
all the dogs at the hotel
for the dogs behind the glass
back and forth back and forth
I have nothing to give them
or the man so utterly broken
standing a little under the scaffolding
his pained voice like a flower
you nearly crush on your way
then I think of Walt Whitman
who told me in his book
to stand up for the stupid
and crazy oh Walt I don't
have any change

I walk down some stairs
to the train where I disappear
into an essay only to emerge
with the train at the canal
the winter sun like a lollipop

a kid dropped in the sky
that's stuck there
an icy-cold action beyond meaning
burning itself up like it's sick
on the inside
an inelegant spray
of unacceptable light
across the city where the essay
still holds power I barely escape
pulling myself out of the train
at my stop my phone waits
to tell me my plans tonight
are exactly like every other night's

then I sleep and just before
I fall asleep a terrible wave
destroys a village smashes the huts
water coming through the woven grass
the kids washed away and drowned
trees stripped down to their skins
and then suddenly like nothing happened
stars come out the water disappears
I get out of the jeep
to buy coconut from a kid
who won't speak she only says
a little cough in her hand

in the bay bright behind her
a great cry from the natives
and the birds sort of swells
to surround us

like the smell of chorizo soup
from the kitchen in their hut
which tasted worse than it should
in the sun while a dream
(I was by now asleep)
said to me that I was
made of love and made of stars
which should be enough for anyone
in a house on the prairie
only waking up when the night
which felt like a blue blanket
and a woman's perfume called me out
to the car and the stars were my guides
because the roads were all straight
out of there driving for hours
through pin oaks without their leaves
like little girls turning themselves away

but the spring is a lie
that is welcome on the trains
everyone's through coughing

and the cardinal is not alone anymore
in a mist and seagulls
sometimes fading out in the clouds
now she speaks to every bird who'll hear her
in the voice of buds opening on every branch
which I hear while I observe
the park entering my constricted lungs
a little break then I breathe it back out
still I feel I can't lose
I see myself in a window
loping like Sasquatch
(this is when I'm still young)
I'm not walking kids to school
not carrying everyone's laundry down the block
around the corner bringing home milk

I risked everything for beautiful hair
now it's gone but I speak now of coconut
shredded in candies
sprinkled on waffles
the roasted kind the street vendors sell with peanuts
its rich milk from a can in a curry
and the chunks sold by girls
on a beach after a wave
washed them away with their brothers

only their ghosts come meet us
when I hop from the jeep
with my money which they accept
though they're ghosts
and the sun on those islands
was so low like I could bat it away

even seeing cars wrecked in trees
trying to cross with my father a stony creek
it was hard to feel haunted in that light
and the lianas indistinguishable from birds
very rare orchids oozing a sap
that transports you a few moments
into the future
or little grains of phosphorescent sand
on the beach

the little ghosts
almost seemed embarrassed
taking my money for the coconut
a whitewashed chapel raised its voice
against the wind
whereas I thought
especially on top of the volcano
the previous morning
it was nature calling the shots

and the wind stirring the palms
was only part of the wind
like a cat flicking its tail
every so often while it sleeps
there is something that's much bigger
than a chapel ringing its bell

and much later pushing N.'s stroller along the park
the Brooklyn winter without even thinking about us here
whips its tail the true winter
is out there like a Russian girl on the train
legs crossed smirking at everything
that's her eye blinding the city
a winter low until the library
blocks it out with the *wisdom that never dies*
carved in gold and we pass
through automatic doors under constant surveillance
from the apartments where the shut-ins watched me smoke
(years before this)
a soggy joint under an umbrella
pushing the stroller
if S. succumbs to the pitter-patter
I remember thinking
I can read the Russian poets
for one hour
like a horse just standing there
while the rain crystallizes over me

in my head there's an argument
about art history
the clouds win
then I see an old man
slowly through rain making his way
with no expression on his face
unless that too is an expression
and I think of elementary school
30 years ago
some of us grow up to become this
very slow man

or the little ghosts by the bay
who sell coconut
the palm trees visible through their bodies

sunlight on the water
like a ship loaded with sequins
has gone down

ARBORETUM

A few words
translated from
nature a little kid in a foreign
spell of anger telling off those
closest to him the breeze comes
up like it's started by the sirens
the sirens chasing the unfortunate
down on the outskirts of town I am
half on vacation mouthing the words
the blithe white butterfly would say
if I were the butterfly

my
wife
lies
beside
me

Bateau!
That's a French kid
excited by the party boat
rolling down the canal lying
underneath this dancing tree
and bubbles from a kid who gets
in trouble my wife smiles and waves it
literally is nothing from a tall
metal tower issues Wi-Fi and
drinking water from the mouth
of a dragon the screams of
children having cramps and
grinning a line forms whenever
the breeze moves a terrier or schnauzer
made of clouds appears and stays

sipping
from
a
small
bottle
of
wine

If you lie still
if you do nothing
everything will be alright some-
one else meticulously grooms
the topiary it must be overnight
while dreaming of a car that
can't fly exactly but is too light
to stay put all the windows
shut the room is painfully
timeless outside 3 drops of
rain fall on the medlar tree
we can hear it sighing I want
to sleep or die but never awaken
and deep beneath the city
the Metro feels the same

while
swallows
bicker
about
who
is
happiest

The reality of this tree is
hexagonal light through the
leaves in others it's a thousand
eyes a little girl wanders away
crying because her mom won't stop
smoking this is on the very edge
of the city summer afternoon
all week the clouds bullied the
sky but backed off someone checks
an extremely loud mic in the park
for a moment I think I'll count
all the bugs in the air pendant
and still green the sweetgum balls
appear to be asleep their time
will come while the swallows
tail each other above the canal
it's hard not to think they're having fun

with
eyes
closed
in
the
sun

Under the spotty shade the
national holiday blazes through
like death is only the beginning
that's what the distant drums
say some of the clouds show
their displeasure or rise up
and the children say that's where
they want to live not me under-
neath a maple tree seasoned with
cumin and cinnamon a cool linen
cloth laid lightly across my future
troubles looking closely at the leaves
they're bitten and sere like a warning
from an old poem something
dark blots the sun

evening
breezes
will
bring
us
even
closer

NATURE POEM ABOUT FLOWERS

Looking back at photographs
our clothes were enormous draped
across our shoulders hanging
low off our hips like they were
someone else's and they were
usually someone's old flannel
it is clear we didn't care
or that we had different goals
for our clothes I remember
one night at the National
Arts Club B. seemed truly shocked
he said *I always pegged you*
as kind of a bohemian
but look at you in that suit
it wasn't unexpected
I drifted through the reading
nursing some very old wounds
acting like I was paying
attention there was somewhere
else I was dreaming about
the dappled and shifting light
of a forest in a book

where the air was cool and smelled
like imaginary flowers
and then we were applauding
and outside on the sidewalk
the city trembled and glowed
and we all felt it beckon
when F. pulled a purple chunk
of opium from his vest
at the bottom of tall streets
at Union Square a flowery
veil descended this was when
the city would wink at us
like it liked us or I thought
approved of us and when
we went to the movies
the actors were dressed like us
and one night it was the night
before I quit a lousy job
I had to get up and walk
it off and when I looked down
at my clothes under a street-
light I saw they were all brown
everything I was wearing
and I heard the phrase *glad rags*
said by someone else
inside my head but also

I remembered the grown-ups
used to talk under their breath
about one of the older
kids how there was something wrong
with him it was obvious
because he only wore brown
and the elders nodded yes
the elders nodded wisely
and I guess I didn't care
because all in brown I stepped
out onto the avenue
—where spring sounded its high notes
and the blue air was perfumed
by all the flowering trees
that people who don't live here
don't believe in, the dogwoods
the redbuds, magnolias
—and I sneezed
and the avenue was lit up
like the deck of a ship
in the morning I would quit
my demeaning job but first
where the electricity
flowed unimpeded I too
wished to flow in my glad rags
through the streets of flowering

night and when I returned home
all the rooms were dark and S.
seemed asleep I quietly
slipped out of my enormous
shapeless clothes and opened
an ancient book trying once
again but without success
to live inside it never
coming out except at night
to finally persuade S.
that we could survive that way
that we could live forever
inside of books and she said
she could agree to part-time
and I said fine and we both
returned to the dreamy dark
that surrounds us but that
we don't share with anyone
and I dreamed I quit my job
by waving a sunflower
at my boss who had no power
over the natural world
and when I woke up I thought
that's not a dream that's just true

SONGS OF WEST RIVER

THE LEADER

The trees do not have a parliament
the birds do not lobby the wind
the moss grows on whatever
side it wants but we
are hideous
blocking out the starlight
and ashamed of this body I sit
on a rock in the middle
of a river and let the sounds
of the water wrinkle around me
through the leaves I see
a bright cloud and I think
that's the leader for me

THE RIVER

An empty field
where some guy used to grow
Christmas trees
now it's filled with sunlight
I'm walking beside

a small river
I am even smaller
there is nothing remarkable
about me

follow the river till
someone says they own it
stand there and watch the river keep going

BONES IN A SOCKET

As in a novel by Thomas Hardy
the trees rub together
like bones in a socket
I hear cars and trucks while
I'm standing in a forest
the little West River sings a song
I sit on a rock in the middle of it
I'm so lucky
most places in the universe
are lifeless and empty

LAVA LAMP

All night I couldn't stop staring at it
the lava lamp giving birth to new worlds
of thick colorful goo rising up
briefly in the spotlight and then falling
back to eventually rise up again
even though it's corny there's a lesson
there, like when the ghost of Lew Welch returns
from the deepest forest to say cycles
are the only thing worth believing in
and sure enough the day has reached the point
where I have to start thinking of feeding
the people I love, the days cycle so fast
one of the cats bats at his water dish
and it rings like a bell, the afternoon
pulls up its collar a bit and darkens
I have done all of this so many times
before, watching massive swords made of clouds
swinging in long slow arcs past the windows
and trapped indoors for most of the winter
putting on records from as far away
as possible and dreaming while awake
flipping listlessly through books of old poems
blowing smoke out the window secretly

what is the argument with myself I
can't stop having, something about life is
not right, it feels like we are all machines
and my mechanism is weakening
I struggle to sit up to drink some tea
so many awful people are healthy
I hear Tim Maia singing *There's no God*
there's no devil, Nobody can live forever
I love that song, it's very uplifting
his mind was temporarily clear then
he could see through the earth into the stars
and there is really nothing there for us
and we should be good to one another
and from the end we should make a brand new
beginning, we should be like the lava
lamp

                              and at this point I was distracted
by the sudden change in the living room
where the long bright fingers of the sunset
turned the actual air a bright orange
and lingering at this moment of change
it seemed that little faeries hovered there
and sparkled and might have something to say.

▪

And then in the midst of all this I dreamed
an enormous navy ship dropped me off
on a beach at night with one other guy
whose identity remained a mystery
the entire time, and we had to watch
the dark cloudy skies for enemy planes
and then we were off, up the beach, driving
through a jungle that was very suburban
and my companion convinced me to break
into one of the houses, and we sat
there in a midcentury ranch-style home
doing nothing and feeling bad about it,
watching their cold lava lamp just sit there
light off, the blobs congealed into one blob,
I said mostly to myself, *There's nothing*
worse, there's no worse feeling than sitting
in the dark in someone's house when they're gone,
and then the guy came home, we could hear him
taking off his coat, throwing down his keys
and I couldn't take it, I cleared my throat
I felt sick to my stomach, I stood up
wearing all white because I am a sailor
and I approached him calmly, I said, *Dude,*
we're sorry, it was just a naval prank
I'm so sorry, I told him, *so sorry*
and we walked up his long jungle driveway

to find his wife in her car, white knuckles
on the wheel, she couldn't get past our car
and expected the worst, and she didn't
believe us, she stared straight ahead sobbing
because she thought we were home invaders
and we were like, *Lady, we're just stupid*
sailors, we swear, and we walked her down there
and it was such a steep and long driveway
we thought, we deserve this, walking back up.

▪

In the morning I went to Prospect Park
to run the 3-mile loop again after
months of being too easy on myself
I feel like I'm being beaten, running,
but you can never stop; the doctor said
Run, boy, run and then she wrote something down
she makes me feel uncomfortable, I smile
I agree to everything, and I run
in the park in the morning and on this
morning the snow was evaporating
fog sat on top of it, all around me
in the ghostly white air the beautiful
drifting soul of the snow filled the morning
and through this thin curtain I had to push
like I was still coming out of my dreams

wondering what is really wrong with me
that my sleeping mind understands, and if
my love has reached her destination yet
slipping through the foggy streets to distant
Queens, where my heart goes
when she goes to Queens.

▪

When I got back I noticed the lava
lamp was still on and it looked kind of dumb
so many things the night makes seem better
even a suburban backyard, magic
is everywhere, in every drop of dew
on the moonlit lawn outside a friend's house
the voices of the trees when the wind blows
but soon you fall asleep, in the morning
everything looks flat, which is how I felt
looking at the lava lamp weirdly spurt
globs of wax upwards, only to fall
back to eventually rise up again
I poured black coffee into a white mug
and read the news, and looked away, confirmed
the mind is a prison and its jailors
are the other prisoners; the morning
as blue as an egg, a delicate veil
of snow quivers on the rooftops across

the street, I see my neighbors through windows
they seem to be keeping busy, and geese
come down like the thin end of winter's wedge.

▪

When my wife decided to take a bath
I sat on the couch trying to work but
thinking of her naked in the next room
with her knees drawn up I was sure because
the bathtub's not that big, and a cat came
and stood on his hind legs and wanted in,
when I close my eyes I see her smiling
and the psychedelic effect that's still there
on closed eyelids like Gysin's Dreamachine
the lava lamp creates, it reminds me
of childhood, dreaming of other planets
but I turned the lamp off, we had to go
we sat in the dark watching *West Side Story*
both of us crying, no one wore a mask
back then, and love like a great bird came
to drape its shadow on the whole city
I took her arm on 14th Street, the cold wind
tried to get between us, we hurried home
bitter out, a bad night to be shackled
belowdecks on the awful prison ships.

THE LITTLE MEN OF THE FOREST

FOR TOMASZ RÓŻYCKI

There are little men in the forest
and I have seen their eyes in the trees
or walking through a sunny clearing
have seen them moving swiftly behind
the forest's edge, moving silently
while the wind tousles the dry rushes
and although that is the only sound
under the sky, indeed the sky is
the sound, it's not even certain
they were there, except for a feeling
behind the eyes that something was moving,
and sometimes beside a creek, voices
make themselves known, lying there you know
you aren't alone, a conversation
creeps up on you slowly, through the trees,
it is the voices of the little men,
the little men who live in the trees,
who sometimes tip loose stones down on you
walking through the narrowest passages
or looking across the creek at dusk
with clouds rolling over the valley

one of the group comes upon a nest
of brightly glowing things shaped like eggs
and who goes right back
to the group to say "Guys, holy shit
you'll never believe what I just saw"
but of course when everyone gets there
the eggs have reverted to just eggs,
and the little men of the forest
are blamed for this too—really, any-
thing mysterious in the forest
is said to be the little men's fault
though some things are clearly different;
if you, for instance, sit by the creek
and do nothing but stare at the creek
the mind is set free, literally,
it has nothing to do, it's boring
to concentrate on a flowing creek
and the mind can do all sorts of things
and if it's given the chance it will
and the side effects of this are great,
a sense of personal well-being,
the distinct feeling that you are one
part of an infinite consciousness,
and this all surely feels magical
and if you can spend an afternoon
this way, by a creek in a forest,

then you have been granted a small glimpse
of something, but something that's nothing
like the little men of the forest;
in the morning, for instance, you might
find, outside your tent, an arrangement
of white stones, and if you try to move
them, even think about moving them,
a feeling will rise up in you
like a storm has risen from the ground,
lifting your hair, and the feeling won't go
until you stop, and you straighten up
and leave the stones, and join the others
at the small morning fire, and tell them
what you saw, and they'll say, "Oh my god,
I had the craziest dream last night
about those stones, and then this morning
when I woke up there was an arrow
made of white stones pointing to my tent!"
or you find large stones piled together
for a ceremonial table
beside a small waterfall somewhere
in the hills and you get the feeling
whoever made it is watching you
though the day, even the waterfall
is suddenly silent, and you know
the little men built this, and watch you,

so you run a hand appraisingly
over its surface, feeling a chill,
then quickly return the way you came
because the little men of the trees
are nobody's friends, except the trees';
what they want is not a mystery,
they want us all out of the forests,
and their presence is, if not dark, then
an ancient magic, and stepping in-
to a clearing where they have just been,
even if it's sunny, is chilling,
and once my wife's brother and a friend
were in a car, very late at night
on Scott Road, a steep, winding road
in Pittsburgh, that passes a graveyard
and both of them saw a little man
run across the road into the trees
and the friend had trouble getting it
out of his head, then later that week
he went to let his dog out, but no,
the dog wouldn't go for some reason,
and growling, backed away from the door
so the friend was like, "What is it girl?"
and peering into the suburban
obscurity he saw the same small
man, a very small man, backing out

of his yard, and he told my brother-
in-law that seeing him twice made him
somehow believe in it even less,
but my brother-in-law was like "No
man, what we saw was definitely
real, don't chicken out" and the friend said
"Chicken out? Fuck you, what do you mean?"
and the conversation continued
like this and we can leave them to it
for they will be at it quite a while,
and we can quietly step away
from them, out of the circle of light
cast by the glowing red lava lamp,
back across the lawn into the trees
where, and I can't speak for anyone
else, but I feel at home, dappled light
playing all across the forest floor,
the hush of steps taken on needles,
the intermittent whoosh of the wind
far above, moving only the tops
of the trees, so the sound seems to be
the trees themselves, not the sound of wind,
this is where I feel comfortable,
because I hate the sun, and I think
if there's any truth to ancestral
predilections that stay in our blood

then I am born of a pale forest
people who liked the sound of raindrops
falling on the canopy above
and who must have known the little men
of the forest, probably leaving
small offerings to them, as I do,
a cookie or a chip on the path
or sometimes a puddle of whiskey
on a rock, which I do all the time
in honor of our twined ancestries
though gaining their favor is a dream
one quickly awakens from,
and sometimes stumbling on a mossy
glade high among the trees I've felt them
nearby, and felt the glow of magic
they must have left behind as they split
when I arrived, but this glow cools down
and soon it turns to a searching cold
that makes the glade uncomfortable
and never again can I find it
which I suppose I can understand
since distilling whiskey is science applied
to plants and I suspect the little
men only want the earthy magic
of fermentation, but I hate beer,
and I remember one time my wife

and I could only afford to share
beers in Iceland because the exchange
rate was ridiculous, and this time
I'm thinking about specifically
we had taken a bus to a small
town that was known to be the center
of the little men's activity
on the island, where construction work
had been halted or roads rerouted
because of mysterious failures
of equipment, drills breaking each time
they bit into the rock or graders
stalling, springing leaks in their fuel lines
and in some cases workers dying
both suddenly while digging the roads
and after work, home in their gardens,
until an old man offered to speak
to the little men of the forest;
3 days later he returned, covered
with pine needles, with wild hair, saying
the little men would cease their attacks
if the city would bypass certain
spots sacred to them, so now the roads
abruptly turn or bypass special
boulders the little men held sacred
and since then they bedeviled the town

no more, and people like me went there
to wander the strangely laid-out roads
by day, seeing nothing magical,
then after a while getting a beer,
such an expensive beer that we shared,
even though I really don't like beer
but apparently a better way
to summon them is to piss them off
snowmobiling through their forest
with 5 of your friends, like Aneke,
a smart, levelheaded young woman
who described an eerie encounter
with the little men, who she called elves,
which happened when she and her friends paused
beside a rocky hillside in
a forest made suddenly silent
after shutting off their snowmobiles;
and while one of them was adjusting
something on the motor and the rest
were drinking from a bottle of schnapps
one of the little men suddenly
appeared beside them, with a bow drawn,
the arrow pointed at Aneke,
all 6 of them saw him; no one said
anything, everyone just staring
at each other, a cold wind blowing,

the little man pulled back on his bow
and a silent agreement spread through
the friends, and back on their snowmobiles
they reversed in a cloud of exhaust
and across the grainy ice they sped,
and when they got to Akureyri
they turned off their motors and said
“What the hell was that? Was that guy real?”
but of course they all knew he was real
and when they reported what they’d seen
the old people of the town all said
they weren’t surprised at all, the little
people hated the way the modern
world encroached upon their way of life
and they agreed that the snowmobiles
were the absolute, most egregious
threat to their realm of timeless magic,
which response caught Aneke off guard
of course, expecting all the grown-ups
to laugh at her or call her a drunk,
but every culture tells the story
of the little men; in ancient Greece
they were called pygmies—not the pygmies
we think of today, African tribes
wearing loincloths, but very tiny
people, a race of people only

a couple feet tall, who were quite brave
and were, according to paintings
on pottery, perpetually
at war with the army of herons;
on one small amphora, recovered
from a site outside Mytilene,
several little men are depicted
tightening a net between grass-blades
to trap, at long last, the heron king
who, at the bottom of the vase, stole
the royal daughter of the small men,
who in a miniaturized scene
was impregnated by the heron
and gave birth to bird-headed children
who, not accepted by the pygmies,
joined forces with cranes and herons
to destroy the race of little men;
the aerial attacks were fearsome
and if the carvings are even close
then it must have been a sight to see,
heron-headed men riding herons
battling very little people
by the shores of the Aegean Sea;
around the lip of the vase are painted
words I couldn't read because they're Greek
but my French is better and since this

amphora was in France, in a town
south of Paris, with a large chateau
that housed a museum of knickknacks
a rich Frenchman plundered, I could read
the translation and it told of how
after the struggle depicted here
the little men fled into the trees,
giving up their life of seafaring
very close to the Aegean coast
and that they lived now as protectors
of the streams and forests and rarely
were they ever seen except by those
who lost their way, and the little men
were said to taunt lost travelers
and pursue them until they wound up
stumbling from the forest, a village
or the shore in front of them, and though
this was helpful in its way, no one
had any illusions about them,
the little people of the forest
have no interest in helping people,
they want nothing to do with people,
and their appearances mark a great rift
in the delicate curtain that hangs
between our world and that of shadows,
through which they pass like the evening wind,

and when they appear, you know something
shadowy is about to happen,
like when I was camping with my friend
in the mountains and after hiking
all day we came to an outcropping
of granite and sat down to relax
and eat trail mix and watch the vultures
making lazy circles in the sky,
and staring into the setting sun
we stopped talking and soon a silence
filled the valley below us and pressed
into our ears, while the sun floated
just above the far peaks, not setting,
and not setting and with an effort
I turned to my friend and said "The sun
isn't going anywhere is it?"
while behind us the trail and forest
were utterly black, as if erased
or as if time passed differently
for us than it did in the forest,
and we slowly rose, gaping and dazed,
unsure how long we'd been sitting there,
when we noticed rocks all around us
that had risen up to become hats
on the heads of dozens of small men
we could only make out because

their eyes glowed bright green and green shadows
stretched out all around us; we yelled "Shit!"
and it sounded like we were yelling
it from the bottom of a deep well;
we had no idea where the trail
lay or how to find it, and our bags
we left behind as we both stumbled
out of the terrifying green glow
into utter darkness and silence,
even our rushing through undergrowth
was noiseless and though branches whipped us
we couldn't feel them, all I could hear
was my own terrified babbling,
all I saw was lights or shapes passing
and in confusion and horror felt
myself stopped by a cold barrier,
and heard a loud dull thud, and felt pain
in my knees and sat down on gravel,
and slowly realized where I was now,
impossibly, I was at my car,
I had run into it, the gravel
was the gravel of the parking lot
at the foot of the mountains, 2 days
from where we'd been surrounded by them,
though our flight felt like it had taken
moments, and looking around I saw

my friend sitting up in the gravel,
the expression on his face bewildered,
and without saying a word we drove
as fast as we could
for it was now daylight.

ARMY OF POETS

JEREMY

Like the Ancient Mariner
stoppeth one of three, now you
are going to hear of my
esteem for crows, the wisdom
and saltiness of the crows
whose use of tools rivals that
of chimps, how crows can think about
crows in the future stealing
from them, and especially
and often do I think of
Jeremy whom Rebecca
knew or a friend of hers knew
on Cape Cod, who was wounded
and dragged his poor wounded wing
across the lawn until she,
whoever this happened to,
wrapped him gently in a towel
and placed him in a small box
and thought to herself—*I know*
there are good-hearted people
nearby who rescue raptors,
and though I don't really know
if crows are raptors, they must

be equipped to take him in,
and so she drove her boxed crow
to them and when she gently
placed the box on a table
a woman removed the lid
and said, exasperated,
Jeremy! and Jeremy
cawed triumphantly and flew
away and did that often
because he liked attention

STILL HAILING IN THE MOUNTAINS

I promised her I'd go out and look
for yogurt it's pouring
I'm thinking
Hundreds of years ago Bashō
walked the roads at night
it rained
The streetlight comes on I close the blinds
I find it
distracting
Lights for Bashō seen through
the wet trees, imagine
how he felt
In one of his poems it's
still hailing in the mountains
when you read it

LOVE POEM (FROM THE ARAN ISLANDS)

December returning
from the Aran Islands
in a storm
in a small boat
belowdecks and I
was singing to you
with your head hidden
your whole body afraid
and later the captain
admitted it was terrible
and you didn't even hear me
the whole trip
my arm around you
the ocean was seething
it was like we were in a song
we were so young
I didn't know what I was doing
stroking your hair
in a little boat

SKYLARK

Siren swinging through
a grey afternoon

I was not born until
dinnertime and I was hungry

a forced and unreal laugh
from the street gets up here

where I am still in bed
after all these years

merrily, merrily have I dreamed
my way outside

my phone keeps dinging
like a skylark in a poem

FOLLOW THEM

Heartbroken over a football game, autumn
evening, of this kind of thing I'm not ashamed
nor of the twistiness of that diction,
or wanting America to burn
though only certain parts deserve to die,
its forests are beautiful and have done
nothing wrong, even the desert's emptiness
is beautiful, though it terrifies me,
and tacos, and kebabs wrapped up in naan,
and today walking through the park I turned
to see dozens of bright white seagulls flocked
on the windy lake against the blue sky
and I felt an ache and I sent a text
to a friend I said TODAY I SAW FLOCKED
ON THE LAKE WHITE SEAGULLS IT WAS BEAUTIFUL
he wrote FOLLOW THEM it was too late

VILLETTE VILLANELLE

Lying underneath a sweetgum tree
in a foreign country under the sun
following the swallows only less free

than they, that's from a poem by Shelley,
too sore to move at all after my run
lying underneath a sweetgum tree

the sun is at its height, she joins me
years later she still thinks I'm the one
following the swallows, only less free

by just a little, like we're all doomed to be,
sometimes her sad face brightens, she says it's fun
lying underneath a sweetgum tree

with the kids, did I mention them? there are three
because we brought the best friend of my son
following the swallows only less free

like everyone in love but with a family
who drifts away from themselves & is stunned
lying underneath a sweetgum tree
following the swallows, only less free

THE PALACE OF JUSTICE

Imagine being hauled
by a few guys
into the Palace of Justice
through the enormous
golden doors oh my
while the sun shines
in every direction
even the innocent
feel guilty stumbling
up those wide marble steps
and the gates so bright
the rest of us look away

FOR A FARRIER

Reading a kind of laborious
poem about rural things
and a horse is shot
for breaking its leg.
I still don't get it.
Surely there's a way
to heal a horse.
I text my friend
who is a farrier
(you know—
someone who shoes horses)
I say surely there's a way
to heal a horse.
                                And I wait
but he doesn't text back
he's busy with the pounding
and clanging.

Raising his hammer
over a bright orange horseshoe
and pausing
because in his head
a line by Issa
can be heard.

POEMS FOR ANNA AKHMATOVA

Your door opened into the heart
of the summer but I had to leave
your place, your husband,
your son, soon they would return.
What were we doing.
You were a tease. We saw Shakespeare
in the Park. Your perfume was too much.
Now I wouldn't even be able to prop
myself up that long, on the cool grass,
waving off with a nod
the little ushers buzzing around
who knew who we were

▪

There is a lost time
when I wore enormous clothes
and all of us triumphed,
as Z. said, by not studying
for the test, and staying out
all night drinking,
and acing it, we triumphed,
this was just a metaphor for our lives,
and in a bar in the daylight

arguing about Russian poets,
I spoke the dread words
that pinned that afternoon
to the wind, and it recedes,
it recedes, and now is so far away
who can really say
if those were the days

■

The evening turns blue out.
Childhood is never very far away.
These Russian poems
in translation are proof.
And they are too heavy
to hold up. I have to put them down.
And when I look in the mirror, my god,
the weight of all these pointless days.
I'm shivering, but I will never
be as cold as you
standing in line
outside the prison
for nothing.

■

According to my watch
I cannot have a drink
yet, instead I breathe

deeply.
The horror of living
in this world of men
is softened by reading books.
And by sleep. To wander
in the crowded bazaars
of a dream, and miss a flight,
and lie in bed with a poet
who cannot stand my poems.
But tossing and turning.
The world is not right.
The river runs softly in the night.

▪

You were even too dark
for the day. When the sun
saw you it hurried past.
And you lay there listening
to the river calling you
out of your bedroom,
into the street, to perch
like a sick bird
on the bridge in the rain.
And you were too goth
for me. I like Frisbees.

POEM FOR CHIKA SAGAWA

A deep and powerful explosion
woke my wife and me, like a tower
of sound it rose from the neighborhood
setting off car alarms. But in the morning
there was nothing, and there was nothing
in the news.
                    Then a ridiculously large beetle
crashed into me and clung
to me. And my undignified efforts
to remove it were useless. It clung
to me, and looked at me closely
while its segmented antennae
sniffed the air. We looked
into each other's eyes.
A great pause came over the world.

THE HEART

I miss you—trapped together though we are
        indoors all year—I dreamed
we disrobed each other—then a child
        entered the bedroom—hello! just floated eerily in
    there was some evil—in her gaze
you pulled on your pants—in another dream
        I reached for something—instead of the kittens
    I touched some awful claw—it woke me
I had fallen asleep—in the posture of one
        who wants to protect his heart

SONNET

Alone in a foreign city
having a drink.
Missing you.
Nursing the drink for a while.
I heard a familiar song
coming over the water.
I said what if we named
our baby Sonnet, later;
at the time you couldn't hear me.
I sat on the dock
underneath vast gantries
and felt an antique crack
in my heart.
But I figured I would make it.

THE MAGIC BOX

When my grandpa died
I got a box
he left behind
filled
with a strange collection
of answers
to very tiny questions
and it never empties
almost 30 years later
4 hooks
solve a little problem
in the cottage
for my daughter
whom he never met
though she has
a little of his surliness
somehow
and if some mere thing
fails her
she sounds just like him
and when she coughs
in the morning
I hear him

dying slowly
and then at a terrible
acceleration
on the highway
with his bird
in the motor home
when he was stricken
and that is when
the box began
to go to work

POEM FOR REGINALD SHEPHERD

Every time I find myself eating
salsa and broken-up chips
with a spoon
I dedicate that act to Reginald Shepherd
who would pull up to a party
late, and do that, and talk
shit about every person
at the table, and I
did not understand why
he wrote so beautifully,
the rest of us thought
we didn't need that
we thought we had put
beauty behind us

POEM FOR LEWIS WARSH

The talk on the playground
is do we let our
kids take the city bus
home from school and why would we
I think we enjoy sitting on the benches
in shallow and repetitive conversation
shifting when the shade shifts
and bad men hang around
4th Avenue the construction sites
attract them I'm just repeating
what the moms say
I'm not listening that closely
I'm trying to work out
how Wordsworth got so square
could it happen to me?

POEM

Woken by wind
I crawled out of the tent
while the little girl slept
and stood on top of a rock
and thought about V.
whom I will never
see again.

A crow came close
and was like,

She's gone!
She's gone!

AN EVENING OF EZRA POUND

Pound, you bastard! —Gerald Stern

I regret appearing
at an evening of Ezra Pound.
I regret that it's searchable online.
I regret our names being together.
I don't regret how I was
kind of mean to the people there
making them feel uncomfortable
at the fancy dinner afterwards
and some of them let's face it
didn't even recognize
Walt Whitman on a button
on my coat, that says it all.
I regret not speaking that evening about
what an asshole he was
how clearly that comes through
how it was the foundation of his poetics.
I regret using "anal rape"
in my bid to make them
uncomfortable at the dinner afterwards.
I do not regret the look on the face
of the famous professor

as I said "anal rape" then tented
my fingers and blithely
slipped it into the conversation
the conversation about the locking up
of Ezra Pound.
I do not regret going to the restroom to run my hands
over my face and text S. that I needed
to escape.
I regret not escaping
through the kitchen—how
fine an act that would be.
I regret leaving my bag at the table
preventing my escape through the kitchen
through the steam and the flames
into the silent alley.
I regret saying his name.
I regret saying his name after
my pinky promise with D.
that we would never say
his name again.

POEM FOR MIROSLAV HOLUB

The Gloomy Octopus lives
inside the book forever

while the teakettle is boiling
I can look into its eyes

and it stares back at me
but does not love me

for it is gloomy, and
the octopus inside the book forever

is made of ink that reflects
light and is reflected in the mind

and what the mind makes,
says Holub, is only there to shore up emptiness

"the primary and secondary emptiness"
which he never explains

GRACE

I hear a rustle and see
a wounded cardinal
in the snowy mud. I have been
drawn to and am looking for
a bagpiper in the cemetery
but pause. Will I have to
put this bird out of its
misery with my boot?
I squat down to it
and speak to it
and it looks at me
and flies away.
A statue dips her shoulder
when I glance at her
but when I go over there
she is still again.
She is Grace S. Folk
and she will be 17
forever.

YEVTUSHENKO WAS THE KING

When the drunk Russian
on the F train pulled out
his flask, people moved
to other seats, but not me.

He said: *You're reading Yevtushenko
in English.* I was. He told me
his father, in the Thaw,
of which Yevtushenko was the king,
wore jeans with battery-powered
Xmas lights up and down the legs.

Do you have to go? he said. I had
gathered my things, we were
at my stop, *I would like to hear
him in English.* I said I'm sorry,
I have to go, and I went
and I'm still going.

NOTES

Friedrich Wilhelm I of Prussia (1688–1740) had an infantry regiment made up of only giant soldiers. I would have just made the cut, which was 6 Prussian feet, or 6 feet 2 inches.

49: written on my 49th birthday; each stanza is made of 49 syllables.

ARBORETUM: if you chop down these 5 trees, a poem remains in the stumps.

NATURE POEM ABOUT FLOWERS: this poem borrows a line from Joshua Beckman.

JEREMY: this poem is for Rebecca Wolff.

FOR A FARRIER: this poem is for Michael Earl Craig.

POEMS FOR ANNA AKHMATOVA: this sequence ends with a borrowing from Dobby Gibson; he likes tennis.

SONNET: this poem borrows a line from Matthew Zapruder.

POEM FOR LEWIS WARSH: this poem is a tribute to Warsh's beautiful poem "For Ten Years," also about waiting outside the school for your kids.

AN EVENING OF EZRA POUND: this poem is for Dara Barrois/Dixon.

YEVTUSHENKO WAS THE KING: this poem ends with the same line that ends Yevgeny Yevtushenko's beautiful long poem "Zima Junction."

ACKNOWLEDGMENTS

Thanks to my readers for their little suggestions that made big differences: Joshua Beckman, Matthew Zapruder, Thea Matthews. To be fair, sometimes the suggestions were big suggestions; thank you, Matthew. Special thanks to Jessica Roeder and Heidi Broadhead for their attentive readings.

Thank you to the editors of the following journals:

The American Poetry Review: FOLLOW THEM, LAVA LAMP, NATURE POEM ABOUT FLOWERS

Conduit: THE LITTLE MEN OF THE FOREST, POEMS FOR ANNA AKHMATOVA

Court Green: 49

Iterant: THE HEART, POEM FOR CHIKA SAGAWA, POEM FOR MIROSLAV HOLUB, SONNET, VILLETTE VILLANELLE, YEVTUSHENKO WAS THE KING

Poetry: FOR A FARRIER, THE HANDOFF

A Public Space: THE PALACE OF JUSTICE

The Round: SKYLARK

Through Lines Magazine: GREENWOOD, PRISONERS

Trampoline: AN EVENING OF EZRA POUND, POEM FOR LEWIS WARSH

AT MY LOWEST POINT, MY NEIGHBOR, and PASSED OVER first appeared in the chapbook *QUADRATIC SONNETS*, published by Copenhagen, 2023.

FOLLOW THEM also appeared on *Poetry Daily* and was selected for *The Best American Poetry 2022*, where it appeared with a maddening printer's error.

POEM FOR MIROSLAV HOLUB also appeared in *Three Hearts: An Anthology of Cephalopod Poetry*, edited by Sierra Nelson, published by World Enough Writers, 2024.

POEMS FOR ANNA AKHMATOVA also appeared on *Verse Daily*.

THE WINTER SUN first appeared in the chapbook *A SHIP LOADED WITH SEQUINS HAS GONE DOWN*, published by Dikembe Press, 2013.